May 1995

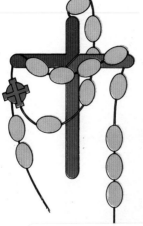

THE
ROSARY

ST PAULS

Original title: *Il Rosario* - © Edizioni AGAM-I 1991
Original text by Renzo Agasso
Designs by Maurizio Boscolo

St Pauls
Middlegreen, Slough SL3 6BT, United Kingdom
Moyglare Road, Maynooth, Co. Kildare, Ireland
60-70 Broughton Road, Homebush NSW 2140, Australia

English edition © St Pauls 1993

ISBN 085439 444 3 (UK)

National Library of Australia Card Number and
ISBN 1 875570 29 2 (Australia)

Printed in the EEC by AGAM, Madonna dell'Olmo (CN), Italy.

St Pauls is an activity of the priests and brothers of the Society of St Paul who proclaim the Gospel through the media of social communication

JOYFUL MYSTERIES
*(Sundays of Advent and Christmas,
Mondays and Thursdays)*

1

The annunciation of the birth of Jesus to Mary

In the sixth month the angel Gabriel was sent by God to a town in Galilee called Nazareth, to a virgin engaged to a man whose name was Joseph, of the house of David. The virgin's name was Mary. Gabriel came to her and said, "Greetings, favoured one! The Lord is with you. You will conceive in your womb and bear a son, and you will name him Jesus."

Luke 1:26-38

If today God were to send an angel to us, would we be prepared to say "yes" as Mary did? Or else would we be answering him, "No, Lord, I cannot, I have so much to do. I would very much like to but you understand me. Not now, maybe in the not distant future." Nevertheless God patiently awaits our "yes" but for how long shall we make him wait?

Lord Jesus, open our hearts to the Holy Spirit and make your home in us.

2

The visitation of Mary to her cousin Elizabeth

In those days Mary set out and went with haste to a Judean town in the hill country, where she entered the house of Zechariah and greeted Elizabeth. When Elizabeth heard Mary's greeting, the child leaped in her womb.

Luke 1:39-42

Mary went with haste to help Elizabeth. Mary could have conveniently ignored the event, and concentrated on her own problems. No, not Mary. She sets out immediately and hurries to the side of this distant cousin of hers in her hour of need. What about us? "How can I think about the others when I am beset with problems of my own?" We prefer to shut ourselves in the cage of our own egoism and in so doing condemn ourselves to loneliness and isolation.

Lord Jesus, give us the spirit of generosity that we may serve you unreservedly in others.

3 The birth of Jesus in Bethlehem

Joseph also went from the town of Nazareth in Galilee to Judea, to the city of David called Bethlehem. He went to be registered with Mary, to whom he was engaged and who was expecting a child. While they were there, the time came for her to deliver her child. And she gave birth to her firstborn son and wrapped him in bands of cloth, and laid him in a manger, because there was no place for them in the inn.

Luke 2:4-8

If today Jesus were to be born again in flesh and blood as then, and if he were to invite us to Bethlehem, would we heed his call, would we believe his words? Some of us may not recognise him. We would perhaps pretend that nothing has happened. We do not physically see Jesus: and yet he is always with us. We would be deluding ourselves if we imagine that we can do without him.

Lord Jesus, be born again in me today, and help me to see you in the world and in all human beings.

4 The presentation of Jesus in the temple

When the time came for their purification according to the law of Moses, they brought him up to Jerusalem to present him to the Lord as it is written in the law of the Lord, "Every firstborn male shall be designated as holy to the Lord".

Luke 2:22-25

We too bring our babies to the church. What is baptism for us: a duty, a social obligation? Or is it a choice of faith, a consecration of our children to God? What have we made of our own baptism?

Lord Jesus, let me first be pruned so that I may bear fruit and witness to the salvation you brought to the world.

5 The finding of Jesus in the temple

After three days they found him in the temple, sitting among teachers, listening to them and asking them questions. When his parents saw him they were astonished; and his mother said to him: "Child, why have you treated us like this? Look, your father and I have been searching for you in great anxiety." He said to them, "Why were you searching for me? Did you not know that I must be in my Father's house?"

Luke 2:46-49

If only we were able to "waste our time" on God! But no: our work, our jobs, our friends, our leisure– all these are for us much more important, much more urgent. The demands of faith can come after them, if there is still some space and time. Our days and years pass by in this manner. We run the risk of reaching the end and find ourselves with empty hands, cold hearts and dead souls.

Lord Jesus, grant me the grace to initiate you in placing your Father's kingdom first.

SORROWFUL MYSTERIES
*(Sundays in Lent,
Tuesdays and Fridays)*

1 The agony in the garden

He came out and went, as was his custom, to the Mount of Olives; and the disciples followed him. Then he withdrew from them about a stone's throw, knelt down, and prayed, "Father, if you are willing, remove this cup from me; yet, not my will but yours be done." In his anguish he prayed more earnestly, and his sweat became like great drops of blood falling down on the ground.

Luke 22:39-46

Every day very many times we feel that we are in the "garden". We do not need much to throw us into fangs of agony and pain. Enough to look around us to see how much of real agony there is: wars, famine, violence and oppression of every kind. Instead of giving ourselves to easy tears, we should dry the others' tears, to soothe their wounds and bring joy and consolation to them.

Lord Jesus, in all our trials and sufferings, teach us to pray that God's will may be done.

2

The scourging at the pillar

Then Pilate asked them: "What do you wish me to do with the man you call the King of the Jews?" They shouted back: "Crucify him!" Pilate asked them, "Why, what evil has he done?" But they shouted all the more, "Crucify him!" So Pilate, wishing to satisfy the crowd, released Barabbas for them; and after flogging Jesus, he handed him over to be crucified.

Mark 15:9-15

We are like the Roman soldiers. We like to flog right and left. We are satisfied with words. But, at times, our flogging tongues hurt more than the whips of those soldiers. How many people have we not hurt with our pride, our jealousies, our false and unkind words?

Lord Jesus, present in all those who suffer, give me the strength to heal broken hearts.

3 The crowning with thorns

Then the soldiers of the governor took Jesus into the governor's headquarters, and they gathered the whole cohort around him. They stripped him and put a scarlet robe on him, and after twisting some thorns into a crown, they put it on his head. They put a reed in his right hand and knelt before him and mocked him, saying, "Hail, King of the Jews!"

Matthew 27:27-31

It often happens that we gloat over the misfortunes of others, especially of our rivals: "It suits him right. He always considered himself above the sorts of us ordinary mortals. Now do you see to what end he has come? Didn't I tell you that his day too would come!" The failures of others are useful to us to take away the limelight from our errors, at times to cover up even our sins!

Lord Jesus, help me to remove a thorn where I can and plant a flower in its place.

4 The carrying of the cross

Then Pilate handed Jesus over to them to be crucified. So they took Jesus; and carrying the cross by himself, he went out to what is called the Place of the Skull, which in Hebrew is called Golgotha. There they crucified him, and with him two others, one on either side, with Jesus between them.

John 19:16-19

We would like to do without the crosses and we are ready to protest: "Lord, why me, what did I do to deserve this now?" But we would not mind heaping one more cross on our neighbour's shoulders. Help the drug addict, the refugees, the poor, those with different personal and social orientation? We don't see it as our duty, we leave it to others.

Lord Jesus, give me strength to deny myself, and take up my cross, and follow you.

5 The crucifixion and death of Jesus

It was now about noon, and darkness came over the whole land until three in the afternoon, while the sun's light failed; and the curtain of the temple was torn in two. Then Jesus, crying with a loud voice, said, "Father, into your hands I commend my spirit." Having said this, he breathed his last.

Luke 23:44-47

Lord, death frightens us. You died in order to give us courage and strength to face our own death. And yet we still tremble at the thought of it, because unlike you we are not able to say: "Father, into your hands I commend my spirit." We are afraid because we do not love you enough.

Lord Jesus, teach me self-abandonment to your Father's love.

GLORIOUS MYSTERIES
(Sundays, Wednesdays and Saturdays)

1

The resurrection of our Lord Jesus Christ

The angel said to the women, "Do not be afraid; I know that you are looking for Jesus who was crucified. He is not here; for he has been raised, as he said. Come, see the place where he lay." They left the tomb quickly with fear and great joy, and ran to tell his disciples.

Matthew 27:5-8

The empty tomb, then those words: "Do not be afraid". To many today the resurrection seems highly improbable, outright impossible. How can a dead person return to life? How shall we be after our death? Though we believe, such thoughts still trouble us. Lord, increase our faith.

Lord Jesus, let me be reminded of your resurrection in every act of forgiveness, trust, friendship, and in our faith which would otherwise be vain.

2
The ascension of Jesus into heaven

Then Jesus led the disciples out as far as Bethany, and, lifting up his hands, he blessed them. While he was blessing them, he withdrew from them and was carried up into heaven. And they worshipped him, and returned to Jerusalem with great joy; and they were continually in the temple blessing God.

Luke 24:50-53

Lord, you are returning to your Father; but we remain here below, beset by suffering and pain. Your promise is to be with us always. But, some days, we feel you are far away, absent and even deaf to our pleas. Lord, you know that we are unable to search for you, to pray to you, to listen to you unless you come to our aid.

Lord Jesus, help me to be a witness to the good news of your kingdom by proclaiming your word and by loving you and my fellow beings.

3 The coming of the Holy Spirit

When the day of Pentecost had come, they were all together in one place. And suddenly from heaven there came a sound like the rush of a violent wind, and it filled the entire house where they were sitting. Divided tongues, as of fire, appeared among them, and a tongue rested on each one of them. All of them were filled with the Holy Spirit.

Acts 2:1-5

The Holy Spirit descended on us too. Has his grace been void in us? Our choices, our words, our actions, our omissions, all seem to say that we are unaware of the Spirit's presence in us. And yet it is an active presence; it leads and guides us, it enlightens and comforts us. The Spirit is always at work in us when we allow him to do so.

Come, O Holy Spirit, and kindle in us the fire of your love.

4 The assumption of the Blessed Virgin Mary

All-powerful and ever-living God, you raised the sinless Virgin Mary, mother of your Son, body and soul to the glory of heaven. May we see heaven as our final goal and come to share her glory.

Prayer from the Liturgy

How is it possible that Mary was taken up to heaven body and soul? We would like it to be the same for us. But we know that is our destiny. Like Mary we too will be taken up to heaven, if we love as she did.

Mother of Jesus, pray for us sinners, now and at the hour of our death.

5

The crowning of Mary and the joy of God's people

Then God's temple in heaven was opened, and the ark of his covenant was seen within his temple. A great portent appeared in heaven: a woman clothed with the sun, with the moon under her feet, and on her head a crown of twelve stars.

Revelation 11:19; 12:1-2

How beautiful it is to think about heaven: God the Father, Jesus, the Holy Spirit, Mary, the saints. We and our dear ones; those whom we have loved and cherished. Is all this only a dream? No, it is not a dream. Jesus assures us of it on behalf of the Father. He preceded us in life, in death, and in the resurrection. That means we too will follow him in life, in death, and in the resurrection.

Mary, my Mother, pray for me that I may one day share in your joy and see the Father in all his glory.

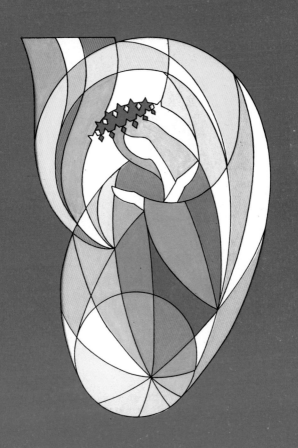

LITANY

Lord, have mercy   Lord, have mercy
Christ, have mercy   Christ, have mercy
Lord, have mercy   Lord, have mercy
God our Father in heaven   have mercy on us
God the Son,   have mercy on us
    Redeemer of the world   have mercy on us
God the Holy Spirit   have mercy on us
Holy Trinity, one God   have mercy on us
Holy Mary   pray for us
Holy Mother of God   pray for us
Most honoured of virgins   pray for us
Mother of Christ   pray for us
Mother of the Church   pray for us
Mother of divine grace   pray for us
Mother most pure   pray for us
Mother of chaste love   pray for us
Mother and virgin   pray for us
Sinless Mother   pray for us
Dearest of mothers   pray for us
Model of motherhood   pray for us
Mother of good counsel   pray for us
Mother of our Creator   pray for us
Mother of our Saviour   pray for us
Virgin most wise   pray for us
Virgin most venerable   pray for us
Virgin most renowned   pray for us

Virgin most powerful	pray for us
Virgin most merciful	pray for us
Virgin most faithful	pray for us
Mirror of Justice	pray for us
Seat of Wisdom	pray for us
Cause of our joy	pray for us
Shrine of the Spirit	pray for us
Glory of Israel	pray for us
Vessel of selfless devotion	pray for us
Mystical rose	pray for us
Tower of David	pray for us
Tower of ivory	pray for us
House of gold	pray for us
Ark of the covenant	pray for us
Gate of heaven	pray for us
Morning star	pray for us
Health of the sick	pray for us
Refuge of sinners	pray for us
Comfort of the troubled	pray for us
Help of Christians	pray for us
Queen of angels	pray for us
Queen of patriarchs and prophets	pray for us
Queen of apostles and martyrs	pray for us
Queen of confessors and virgins	pray for us
Queen of all saints	pray for us
Queen conceived in grace	pray for us
Queen raised up to glory	pray for us
Queen of the rosary	pray for us
Queen of peace	pray for us

Lamb of God, you take away the sins of the world

have mercy on us

Lamb of God, you take away the sins of the world

have mercy on us

Lamb of God, you take away the sins of the world

have mercy on us

V. Pray for us, O holy Mother of God
R. That we may be made worthy of the
promises of Christ

Let us pray

O God, whose only begotten Son, by his life, death and resurrection, has opened to us the rewards of eternal life; grant, we beseech you, that, meditating upon these mysteries, in the most holy Rosary of the Blessed Virgin Mary, we may imitate what they contain and obtain what they promise. Through Christ our Lord. Amen.

PRAYERS OF THE ROSARY

(Each decade of the rosary is composed of one Our Father, ten Hail Marys and one Glory be to the Father. The rhythm of the prayers is to help us to grow in contemplation.)

In the name of the Father, and of the Son, and of the Holy Spirit. Amen.

●

O God, come to our aid.
O Lord make haste to help us.

●

I believe in God, the Father almighty,
    creator of heaven and earth.
I believe in Jesus Christ, his only Son, our
    Lord.
      He was conceived by the power of the
        Holy Spirit and born of the Virgin
          Mary.
      He suffered under Pontius Pilate,
        was crucified, died, and was buried.
      He descended to the dead.
      On the third day he rose again.
      He ascended into heaven,
        and is seated at the right hand of the
          Father.

He will come again to judge the living and
the dead.
I believe in the Holy Spirit,
the holy catholic Church,
the communion of saints,
the forgiveness of sins,
the resurrection of the body,
and the life everlasting. Amen.

•

Our Father, who art in heaven, hallowed be thy
name. Thy kingdom come. Thy will be done on
earth, as it is in heaven. Give us this day our daily
bread, and forgive us our trespasses, as we
forgive those who trespass against us, and lead us
not into temptation, but deliver us from evil.
Amen.

•

Hail, Mary, full of grace, the Lord is with thee.
Blessed art thou among women, and blessed is
the fruit of thy womb, Jesus. Holy Mary, Mother
of God, pray for us sinners, now and at the hour
of our death. Amen.

•

Glory be to the Father, and to the Son, and to the
Holy Spirit, as it was in the beginning, is now, and
ever shall be, world without end. Amen.

Hail, holy Queen, mother of mercy; hail, our life, our sweetness and our hope! To you do we cry, poor banished children of Eve; to you do we send up our sighs, mourning and weeping in this vale of tears. Turn then, most gracious advocate, your eyes of mercy towards us; and after this our exile, show to us the blessed fruit of your womb, Jesus: O clement, O loving, O sweet Virgin Mary.

●

Eternal rest give unto them, O Lord.
And let perpetual light shine upon them.
May they rest in peace.
Amen.